T0146420

DANCING
IN HER OWN *Full*
MOONLIGHT
THE EBB AND FLOW OF BEING FULLY WOMAN

JANELLE FLETCHER

BALBOA.
PRESS

A DIVISION OF HAY HOUSE

Balboa Press books may be ordered through booksellers or by contacting:

Balboa Press
A Division of Hay House
1663 Liberty Drive
Bloomington, IN 47403
www.balboapress.com.au
1 (877) 407-4847

Because of the dynamic nature of the Internet, any web addresses or links contained in this book may have changed since publication and may no longer be valid. The views expressed in this work are solely those of the author and do not necessarily reflect the views of the publisher, and the publisher hereby disclaims any responsibility for them.

The author of this book does not dispense medical advice or prescribe the use of any technique as a form of treatment for physical, emotional, or medical problems without the advice of a physician, either directly or indirectly. The intent of the author is only to offer information of a general nature to help you in your quest for emotional and spiritual well-being. In the event you use any of the information in this book for yourself, which is your constitutional right, the author and the publisher assume no responsibility for your actions.

Print information available on the last page.

ISBN: 978-1-5043-0539-6 (sc)
ISBN: 978-1-5043-0540-2 (e)

Balboa Press rev. date: 12/08/2016

Thirty days of poetry over a lunar cycle
and daily reflections for you

to help you find peace
through the joys and challenges
of being a woman, mother, or lover

and

to find and fuel your feminine;
fiercely love yourself,
your body,
your ebb and flow,
and to be fully woman
as you navigate your transitions in life.

Dedicated to

my six beautiful children,
Amy, Gemma, Sophie,
Josh, Hannah, Levi,

and to the men and women in my life
who have heard me cry in my darkest hours,
urged me on when I have doubted,
celebrated my successes,
and seen the beauty, love, and courage
within my spirit.

I honour you all for

hearing me,
seeing me,
loving me.

Contents

Praise

Janelle writes from the depth of her soul's pain, the rawness and honesty providing a cloak of comfort and community for those who feel they too are alone. *Dancing in Her Own Full Moonlight* is a beautiful, heartfelt gift for those upon the path of womanhood with its many transitions and challenges. It gives reassurance and a knowing that you are seen, you are heard, and you are not alone.
—**Debbie Gillespie, wise woman,** www.debbiegillespie.nz

Janelle Fletcher brilliantly creates a journey into herself without leaving home, writing at dawn for thirty days, allowing what comes to arise within her and find its way onto the page. She inspires us to find our own way to truly and deeply receive ourselves and this life we are given.
—**Oriah "Mountain Dreamer" House, author of** *The Invitation,* www.oriah.org

Janelle's raw and honest poetry speaks to the silent struggles of a woman emerging into the light and offers comfort and solace to others in times of transition.
—**Christine Sheehy, Write to the Heart of Your Business,** www.christinesheehy.co

I'm loving these heartfelt poems written by Janelle. They speak to me deeply, amplifying the whispers of my own feminine soul and calling me to deeper rest, deeper self-love, and the recognition that from this place, goodness can radiate and flow out effortlessly to nourish, soothe, and even heal the aching heart of humanity. The questions at the end of each poem are simple invitations to go deeper and unveil what has

been peeking out from behind the worldly mask and whispering for attention. It's a book to be picked up regularly as a simple daily reflective practice.
—**Katrina Stadler, friend, artist, and kindred spirit**

Janelle Fletcher offers us a wonderful guide for connecting with the moon that lives within. *Dancing in Her Own Full Moonlight* takes the reader on a cyclical journey of inspiration, inquiry, and reflection and shines a gentle light on what it means to be woman.
—**Anita Johnston, author of** *Eating in the Light of the Moon,* www. dranitajohnston.com

Using writing as a tool, practice, or prayer to journey back to your true self has always been my very favourite kind of medicine to share with women in circle, which is why I'm giving Janelle Fletcher massive high-fives and deep bows of reverence for not only daring to hear my call, but for being willing to go there and share what she wrote in our thirty days together. Janelle's words are true, real, and raw, and when we share stories from this place, other women can see their own truths reflected back at them. Thank you for being our mirror, Janelle!
—**Lisa Lister, author of** *Code Red, Love Your Lady Landscape* **and** *Write Your Freakin' Heart (and Guts) Out programme,* www. thesassyshe.com

"In your silent womanly struggles,
there is an invitation to greater self-love, body honouring,
and connecting to your feminine spirit."

www.janellefletcher.com

Preface

The Beautiful Moon

It is with heartfelt thanks that I honour a soul sister, Lisa Lister, with whom I shared thirty days of writing. Lisa was my gorgeous guide and listening post. She saw me and she heard me. She held the space for me and she invited me to follow the beautiful, empowering phases of Mother Nature, our lunar and menstrual cycles, which offer us women the privilege to

- recreate balance in our lives on a daily, monthly, and seasonal basis.
- shed parts of ourselves that require healing.
- sit with our pain in the dark night of the soul.
- restore and re-energise ourselves.
- venture forth and create new things with confidence, all in sync with the phases of the moon.

In the richness of ritual each morning for thirty days, in Lisa's words, I "rifted my heart." With no starting or ending point in mind, over sixteen thousand words graced my page as I connected, channelled, and flowed with what revealed itself each dawn.

Dancing in Her Own Full Moonlight flowingly revealed herself as the unsilencing of my voice I had kept quiet and hidden for too long. It is my soul's cries, yearnings, real and raw creative expressions, and outpourings of the highs and lows of womanhood, motherhood, and loverhood, as well as my path to being fully me in my ebb and flow.

I discovered that my very intuitive time was 5:30 in the morning—an hour when I was not accustomed to being awake, but it was one in which I discovered the depth of my creative juices, the pining of my soul, the cries of desperation for something different, and a deep appreciation for what and who has been part of my life to date.

I healed many aspects of my past at a very deep, visceral level and gained new perspectives on what was previously difficult and painful. This healing has restored and re-energised my spark - my *joie de vivre* - and what is now manifesting in my life.

It was also in this still time each day that I got new clarity on my purpose for living and the signposts for my emerging life - one as poet, storyteller, healer, wise woman, feminine spirit guide, and a femme extraordinaire continuing to love myself.

Dancing in Her Own Full Moonlight is my gift to you.

It is my hope that my unedited poetry rifted each morning from my heart to yours resonates, rejuvenates, and reminds you of your deeper, richer, and amazing self. It is an invitation for you to love yourself in your amazingness and messiness, in your highest of moments and darkest of days, your confident highs and self-doubting lows, your dreams and your unfulfilled goals, and your feeling beautiful and your less than self-loving moments.

It is also an invitation for you to be still, hear your own whispers, shouts, and bloodcurdling screams, and creatively express them in the way that is unique to you. It is an opportunity for you to also find the deep connection within, dance to your own rhythm again, ignite your passion, and find you again amidst the hustle and bustle of a busy life and your constant giving to others.

Enjoy the poetry each day and consider the reflection questions as a starting point for your journey ahead. Share them whenever and wherever you find yourself with kindred spirited women. Create a circle, a support group, a network, a writing group—whatever supports you to express yourself and shine through the lows and highs of being a woman, mother, and lover. You may find further inspiration, support, and women's empowerment programmes at www.janellefletcher.com.

May you continue to bud, blossom, die, and grow again in the gloriousness of being fully woman, gifted by the lessons of nature and our cycles.

Introduction

Invitation to Love

"Let the light of love that you are express herself fully."

Soul sister, my soul yearns for you to find a different way than the self-sacrificial path you are on.

My soul cries for you to learn that is it okay to be you in your fullness, not just in the "smile on your face" moments when you feel like you need to be all to everyone and everything except yourself.

It is time, darling, for you to stop prioritising others' needs, start thinking about you and finally accept the invitation to have self-care as your soul reason for getting up in the morning.

Gorgeous, can't you hear the soft whisperings or the loud banging at your door?

- Your body is crying out for you to be kinder to her, honour her, and love her.
- Your mind is begging you for a retreat where you think of no one and nothing else, and which allows the whispers of your soul to be heard above your mind chatter.
- Your spirit wants you to finally feel that you are enough and that you are not alone. Connecting to your feminine spirit will make you feel alive again.
- Your inner well is crying, "I'm dry and depleted and need refreshing."
- The tough time, change, or transition you are experiencing right now is your wake-up call to finally get you out of your cage and fly again!

But the truth is this.

- We women are typically over-doers and over-givers, and we hold everything and everyone together while we are often crumbling apart.
- We are often tamed, responsible, and serious when all we want to do is play, be pleasured, and live a wildly exciting life.
- We are often at war with our niggling self-doubt and lack of time and energy while trying to get ahead in life and live our purpose.
- We want to love our changing bodies but continue to criticise, compare, or chastise them.
- We keep our emotions and grief under wraps, and we keep ploughing through the best we can.
- We are desperate for love but throw away intimacy by being too busy, distant, or distracted.
- We remain unhealed and silenced, and our soul is dying knowing there is more to life than constantly doing and giving unto others.

Does this feel like you?

Gorgeous, it is now time

- to give to you and put yourself up the priority list.
- to be more real and raw.
- to love your body and yourself.
- to feel energised—physically, sexually, soulfully and creatively.
- to enjoy more pleasure.
- to heal your past.
- to be unsilenced, speak your truth and be heard.
- to honour your soul and beautiful feminine spirit.
- to have self-love and self-care as your natural way of being.
- to be fully woman in all of your glorious amazingness and messiness.

It's time, dear one, for you—your ever-beautiful, ever-playful, and ever-luscious self

**to show her face, to dance in her body,
and to feel free in her spirit.**

- But what is within us women that has us feeling like we are not enough?
- What is it that keeps our every waking moment thinking of others well and truly before ourselves?
- What is it within our spirits that drives us to sacrifice our real passions and purpose?

My life to date has been answering those questions, and I have been gifted many lessons in the art of self-love, self-validation, and self-care.

Every life lesson, difficult experience, change, or transition has taken me deeper, broader, and wider into realising that it is not striving for a bigger and better life that is my success in life. It is as simple as loving me in all of my fullness—my greatest of days and my grottiest, the very confident, moving-ahead moments and the days that I hardly lift a finger, or the days where I feel gorgeous, and the days when I don't. Everything is well in that rich landscape of life's experience. That is life, and therein lies my learning, my lessons, and my invitation to love.

- What transitions have taught me that outer success is transient, and inner peace is my success during difficult times?
- What experiences have humbled me to my darkest moments, but which have also allowed me to fully capture the power of self-love and allow my feminine spirit to shine?
- What painful times have allowed me to fully connect to the beauty of my body, the enormous love in my heart, and the loud longings of my spirit to claim that I am enough as I am?

I have always felt different. I have often felt not good enough. I have never fully found my place of belonging, and I am an over-giver. My life lesson has been to see my uniqueness, my courageous spirit, the solace I find in my inner life, and my generous heart as beautiful gifts.

My strict religious upbringing has allowed me to value the contrast of religion and the spiritual connection and freedom that I now enjoy with my inner divinity.

After losing my favourite grandmother, the grief which I deeply felt but hid has gifted me tears, compassion, and a huge heart for those going through such loss.

My eleven-year experience of loathing my body, anorexia, bulimia, and disconnection from the amazingness and beauty of my body led me down a dark path to a suicide attempt. That was my wake-up call to say, "Enough is enough." I have chosen self-love ever since because it is my sole (and my soul's) choice.

Marrying into a "ready-made family," a widower with three daughters, was a natural and instantly recognised next part of my soul's journey. A visit from my husband's wife in spirit was my first awakening and appreciation that we have soul helpers. This beautiful soul entered me into the marriage and family dynamic, which was divinely orchestrated for its time, reason, and season. Like a soul sister (or in our case, soul mothers), I could not have done this passage of time without her, and I honour her for that.

My desire to have babies and my subsequent years of infertility and miscarriages were gifts to help me get more in touch with my body, its rhythms, the moon phases, and the beliefs, emotional undertones, and grief that were impacting my fertility and soul purpose of becoming a birthmother. I am incredibly grateful that the honour of motherhood was bestowed upon me, and I now have six beautiful children, most having now flown the nest.

My many years of being a mum has heightened my fervent belief that as mothers, we need to honour the special time and blessings of motherhood despite the tiring, terrible, and daunting moments we can sometimes experience. Joy for me is being present with my children and being love to them. My learning now, however, is to love myself first in order to be an even better mother.

Waning intimacy in my relationship caused my partner and me pain. Intimacy is at the core of our being, but it is one of the hardest aspects of ourselves because it often requires us to feel vulnerable, exposed, embarrassed, shamed, and alone. That is ironic as intimacy is our greatest gift into love.

Betrayal from family members has hurt me, and I have learned that being comfortable as a black sheep, finding my voice, and being true to myself is part of my personal duty and honour in this lifetime.

Being humbled financially has taught me it is my inner riches that put a smile on my face, not my outer riches. Love wins every time. Family get-togethers lift my spirits. Being generous is wealth in itself. Having a charitable heart is honourable.

Meeting soulmates and instantly recognising them has left me feeling, "I'm a lucky girl." However, soulmate relationships are not sugar and spice and all things nice. They are challenging, joyful, terrifying, and blissful—an interesting concoction of soul growth opportunities.

Now that I'm entering menopause, I am learning a far greater emotional spectrum, from deep highs and heightened, even explosive emotional states to deep lows and soul-questioning moments. This transition, much like the chrysalis and emerging butterfly, is requiring me to let go of others' needs as my priority and honour my needs and what would bring me pleasure, love, joy, peace, and a deep inner smile. It is asking me to honour my own rhythm and slow down. It is inviting me to dance in my own full moonlight again and not march to the beat of someone else's drum.

I trust that you enjoy the thirty days of poetic channelled wisdom, words, and utterings from deep within my well, and that they resonate deeply within your spirit and spur you on to live a more truly authentic life, to be more real, raw, and ravishing, and to ride the ebb and flow of life rather than fight against it. That is where the feminine lies.

Dark Moon—Earth—Winter

*"In the depth of my darkness, I patiently
discovered light as the winter faded."*

Graceful Success

Abundant Inadequacy

Lady in Waiting

Let It Go

Homeless and the Homecoming

Day 1

Graceful Success

I don my cloak of mana,
Gifted by a wise woman friend.
Black and red feathers
A symbol,
A promise.

I feel my mana,
My powerful woman presence—
Strength,
Leadership,
And feminine grace—
Reveal itself from under her cloak.
Unknown where the journey is taking me,
But knowing
In all of my knowingness
It is somewhere
Profound.

❖ How does the world define success?
❖ What personal values would you prefer to live your life by?
❖ How can you live more gracefully while trying to succeed in the world?

Day 2

Abundant Inadequacy

Today I awoke
To the prompt of "Honour rest; do nothing."
Interesting
As I am overwhelmed with impending work, family stuff,
And upcoming Christmas,
And a feeling I will miss the boat
If I do not honour my commitment I made just yesterday
To rise early and write,
And finally reveal some of
My words,
My wisdom
To the world.

Reprieve
From my feeling of abundant inadequacy,
But that is what the dark moon
Offers me today.
Time to be more in my darkness
And the warmth of my bed,
And to know that I am truly
Not inadequate.

I just need the rest
To re-energise my spirit
And rebalance society's needs,

Giving to my family, my business, my community,
And my own soul's needs.
Giving the gift
Of time,
Attention,
Rest,
And love
To me.

❖ In what areas of your life do you feel inadequate?
❖ What is the cost of constantly giving to others and leaving yourself depleted?
❖ What are the benefits to you and others for "honouring rest and doing nothing" more regularly?

Day 3

Lady in Waiting

Lady in waiting.
A pregnant woman
Expectant with her unborn child,
Formed to perfection
But not fully developed yet.
I am not yet born,
But am about to be.

Always in waiting,
Broken promises,
Unfulfilled dreams
Shattered before birthed,
Or gifted at the final hour.

I am about to give birth
After many long weeks and trimesters.
False labour pains have prepared me for the birth.
The true labour pains have begun
And are almost strong enough now
For me to push the child into this world
And be relieved of the waiting
And have promises fulfilled.

The push, however, comes not from the midwife or the husband
Who supports me, the groaning woman,
But comes from deep within

As I flow with the ebb and tide of contractions
And push not with will and might,
But only when my body urges me to.

Time has come to give birth
Not to my child,
But to my new self.

- ❖ What aspects of your life require you to be more patient at the moment?
- ❖ What are you now wanting to birth within yourself? Creativity? Self-love? Adventure? Intimacy?
- ❖ How can you allow your natural body rhythms and the timing of Spirit to help birth these things into being?

Day 4

Let It Go

What do I let go of
In my womanly generational umbilical cord,
That continues to bind me and entangle me in
Busyness, responsibility, and self-sacrifice?

What is it within my veins that calls me to action,
Propels me into doing,
And keeps my well of energy depleted?

Women of my line,
I let go today not of you,
But of the lineage of that which keeps us slaves to others,
Sacrificial lambs
And self-care depleted.

Compassion for others flows,
In fact, throbs through our arteries
As a lineage of caring women,
But arteries are bigger than veins.

Where is the venous return
That re-energises our compassion,
Pure compassion
Unadulterated
By the deep desire

To be validated,
Noticed,
Loved?

Let us stay connected as woman of lineage.
But today I choose to
Cut the cord
Of that entanglement,
Tendency,
Vow.

And the angst that I feel
When I notice
My daughters,
My sons
Reacting to my emerging self-care
And my own reaction
To their self-care practices
That break heavily away
From what I have
Fervently
And with purpose
Wanted to pass on to them.

I realise that it pains me
But that pain
Is the cry
For the severing of that vow,
That umbilical cord,
And that tie
To selflessness.

❖ What disempowering patterns and behaviours do you notice in your generational line?

❖ What can you do intuitively today to cut that cord and create a different legacy?

❖ How can cutting that cord impact not just your future generation, but your past?

Day 5

Homeless and the Homecoming

I remember coming home
To my house of childhood,
Key downstairs,
Waiting to be fetched to let ourselves in.

Unusual because my mum was always there,
But in this instance, she wasn't.
She had started working
But would no doubt return soon after
To see part two of her day begin:
The cooking of the family meal.

Home was an open place for friends,
Strangers, young ones, churchgoers,
And others to assemble,
To be fed well,
And to enjoy some hearty times together.

My home too has been a place
That is open
To travellers, wayfarers,
Exchange students,
Women's gatherings,
Friends of kids,
Birthday party attendees,
And most of all my brood of kids.

But has it been open
When those whom I treasured most
Left the nest
Or were sent away
By me
In my stifling need for
Self-preservation,
Self-care and ease?

The martyr does not offer a home for free.
She offers with some conditions
That may or may not be met.

Did I do my children a disfavour
By the way I was mother and offered home?
Was it not cosy enough for them to want to rest a while there,
Knowing it was a comfortable place to stay?

My heart broke into pieces as I watched our second
Wheel out the door and into no woman's land
To live life on her terms
And fend for herself
In what looked like
The darkness.
But there is joy
In seeing what has come to light
For her.

And our first,
We thought, was old and wise enough
To conquer the world on her own,
As well as allow us space
To provide home
To the younger ones,
Who now required the time and attention

That we had for so long offered her.
But pain for a mother whose nest was emptying,
Minus this beautiful soul at home,
And for a daughter whose decision it was not.

And I faced yet again
The pain that came when our third
Quietly left home with her belongings.
Me, unaware.
Me, completely sorrowed.
But she ventured into the world
That she had courageously chosen.
But what had I missed?
What was my lesson?
Was I so awful to be around?
And how could she be mothered by another
In the way that I hoped she would be
Mothered by me?

And if that was not enough,
My son's own choice
To honour his call as a young teen,
To find home within his father's arms
In a far-off land,
Left an even emptier nest.
But a chick knows there is always a nest to return to,
And a mother bird finds pleasure
In seeing her bird fly confidently
In the winds of change.

And as I take a glimpse
At how number five is gypsying
As an emerging woman
To her siblings and friends more often,
It is perhaps the beginning of her own

Emergence into self
And life discovery
And flying the nest.

And as I think of my youngest
And what a solo child might feel one day,
I am saddened
For the quietness,
The loneliness,
And perhaps the boredom and unease
Of living with parent
But not with siblings.
As youngest,
I cry that he has not experienced family
Or home
As I would ever hope
Or dream for my children.

So, where and what is home for me?
I have not returned to my home for years,
And I wonder if
I would have to put on my straitjacket
Of fitting in to be accepted,
Silence my voice
For fear again of being misheard,
Stifle my vitality
For fear of being seen as crazy,
And feel the discomfort
Of conversation being created
For the sake of breaking the deafening silence
Of lack of connection.

I have not been attached to house
Or country,
But in my aloneness

All my life,
Where I have felt invisible,
Unwanted,
A nuisance,
Different,
I have carried
My shell with me,
Perhaps seen by others
That this home is too small
For them to also reside in,
To cohabitate,
Or to be sheltered from the worries
Of the outside world.

Homecoming has been my quest
For both me and for my kids.
They may not have always found that within my walls
Despite my attention,
Affection,
Intention,
But I am loving the return
Of family
When they knock on my door
Or share their own homes now
With me.

One day soon I will don my backpack
And venture forth again
As my own free spirit in the world
Of home
And non-attachment to others,
But in full attention of myself:
My own needs, comforts, pleasures,
And my own peace and ease
In my heart

That feels like
A hearth, a fire,
And the warmth of feeling
Loved,
Seen,
Me.

- ❖ What has been your experience of house and home?
- ❖ What would it feel like in your body if you were at home with yourself?
- ❖ How can you experience that feeling right here and right now?

Waxing Moon—Air—Spring

"As I breathed a new breath, I began to find spring within me."

The Swing in My Step

Out Cold on the Bathroom Floor

Pipped at the Post

Judgement Day

My Truth Unsilenced

Never Alone

The Ink Floweth

Conception Moon

Day 6

The Swing in My Step

Help me get the swing back in my step,
The tango back in my feet,
And the charleston happening in my spirit—
Not the nervous novice on the stage
About to do her impromptu
Or debut,
But someone who knows her competence
Even in the unfamiliar,
Ready to enlighten,
Entertain,
And equally dance with joy.

- ❖ What does life feel like today? A graceful ballet step, head-banging mosh, seductive tango, cheeky charleston, or a slow foxtrot?
- ❖ Is your body asking for a different dance, intensity, or change of pace?
- ❖ How will you honour what your body is telling you?

Day 7

Out Cold on the Bathroom Floor

Last night I slew the dragon.
I fainted on the bathroom floor.
Memories of childbirth
And the atrocities I have witnessed
In my many lives,
Having cut the umbilical cord this week
To mothering as I have known it,
To the generational lineage of
Service and sacrificial lamb,
And to the sucking of energy
That occurs when I
Connect and care for people.
It feels apt that
I died to my old life,
Waking up on the bathroom floor
Not knowing where I was,
In unfamiliar territory
And feeling a little worse for wear.

- ❖ What is your body and energy level telling you today?
- ❖ What is dying within you? How can you, in ritual, allow that death to occur?
- ❖ What new life is pining within you to have expression? How can you breathe life into that?

Day 8

Pipped at the Post

My puberty memories
Showed me always lagging in the race
To fully become woman.
Always pipped at the post
For the prize
Of first bleed,
First breast buds,
First boyfriend,
First kiss,
First sexual encounter,
First being pleasured
And seen as desirable.

There was always some other
Femme fatale
Who would ruin my race,
Wear the medal,
Claim the bragging rights,
Squeal with delight,
Or proudly fashion her tightest of jeans,
Most buxom of bras,
Or something that looked anything different
From my more asexual-looking attire,
Uniform, or sports clothes.

I did, however, attract the attention
Of older men
Who saw the more internal me,
The talent, strength, intelligence,
And feist within my spirit.

Is that why
I ventured headstrong into academia?
To hide from my feelings
Of not being woman,
Not being desirable,
Or not even being allowed
To show my face of femalehood
In a largely ordered
And religious world
In which I had
To live
To conform,
And which allowed me
To hide my hurt feelings?

Is that why I chose to venture
To the other side of the world?
To escape
And attempt to give
Expression to my feelings,
Find sensuality in my soul and
Freedom in my movement,
And womanliness
In my veins,
In my heart,
Sexual self,
And in my Being?

It was only through life
And what she gifted me
In the pain of anorexia and bulimia,
Deep darkness,
The hotel room,
Infertility,
Loss of child,
Taking on babes as my own,
Pregnancy,
Birthing,
Motherhood,
And the countless woman whom I have helped
Come through their own
Womanly transitions,
Changes,
Uncertainty,
Self-doubt,
Body disconnection.

All of this has gifted me the way
To my womanhood:
The beauty of it,
The pain,
The pleasure,
And the mundane,
But mostly the joy of loving
My body,
Myself,
My ebb and my flow,
And comfort within my skin—
The freedom and joy
Of being fully woman.

There is no better prize than that,
And I happily run
That race every day,
Knowing there is
No winner,
No pipping at the post,
But a journey of other women
Simply finding themselves.
Each learning to embrace life
As a gorgeous, gifted,
Hot, powerful,
Emotional, and content woman,
Happy to be in the skin she's in
And loving the joys
Of being female.

- ❖ How did your experience of puberty shape your life as a woman and your respect or disrespect for your body?
- ❖ What body changes, transitions, or losses have left you feeling powerless? How have they also empowered you?
- ❖ What simple act of kindness can you do today that will show new respect for your body?

Day 9

Judgement Day

To be seen
For who I am
Has paid its toll
Within the ranks.
The judgement:
Unfair,
Unjustified,
Wrong.
Not guilty
Of prostitute,
Negligent mother,
Hopeless businesswoman,
Depressive,
Failed wife,
Controlling,
Heartless.

The gavel falls.

❖ How are you one of your biggest judges? What has judgement and criticism stopped you from doing or being?
❖ Whose opinions of you do you let rule your life?
❖ What would it take to be strong enough to listen to your own inner truth of good-enough-ness?

Day 10

My Truth Unsilenced

What truth would I reveal
If I dared voice what has been hidden,
Ignored,
Or denied a listening ear?

The medical system let me down.
It was uncaring and insensitive
And left me disempowered,
But equally detoured me to the path of more
Enlightened,
Body-connected
Ways of enjoying health
And empowerment.

I was born into religion,
But this squashed me
Into something I wasn't.
Spirituality is allowing me
To be more the real, expansive me
Without being chastised,
Judged,
Or condemned.
Herein lies
Freedom.

Betrayal, when it happens
Within one's circle of women,
Is damaging to one's spirit.
Women equally hold the power, however,
To be the most loving beings
And change the world positively
When they believe in
And support each other.

Motherhood is a blessing,
But is also a great means of learning the lessons
Of loving unconditionally
Without any return of favour.
The more one values motherhood,
The more she may be disappointed
If she seeks validation
Outside of herself.

Busyness
Is not what it's made out to be.
External measures of success are fleeting
When compared to success from the inside of
Self-love,
Connectedness,
Contribution,
Peace,
Love.

Women are born beautiful.
Women are beautiful.
Women will always be beautiful.
We are curvaceous beings,
Ebbing and flowing
With imperfections and perfections,
Giftedness and grottiness,

Smiles and huge sobs of tears,
Aspirations and lack of follow-through,
A desire to be equal
But equally desiring to be princesses.

We are not straight lines.
Neither do we succeed more by
Hiding our curvaceous nature
Behind a veil of success,
Accomplishment,
And getting shit done.

It is ironic that
Women have been silenced
And made into driving and striving machines
By their own choice
Or outside forces,
But have the power
Within their truth
To ignite a revolution
To alter humankind's actions
And to change the world
For good.

For this, however,
We need to allow women to be beautiful women
And bring the feminine—
Still,
Sacred,
And soulful—
Into the everyday living of
Their daily lives.

❖ What is your truth that you have kept silenced for too long?

❖ What effect has dampening your truth had on your body, health, and relationships?

❖ What positive impact could giving a voice to your truth have on you and others?

Day 11

Never Alone

Too many people go it alone
And miss the knowing
That they are not alone,
Not unseen,
Not unsupported.

Within us and around us
Is the abundance of things unseen,
But definitely felt
And recognised
From deep within
When connected to that source of abundance.

Our connection
To spirit,
To nature,
To love
Gives us our day-to-day,
Practical guideposts
Without the angst
Of working it out.

It gifts us
The support crew
Who will hold us
When things get tough,

And who will also whisper
Or even shout to us,
"Keep going!"

We need not fear death,
Our own or others,
Because you and they are not gone.
They are forever connected,
Accessible,
Available,
And on tap
To draw courage,
Strength,
And insight from.

❖ Who is your support crew (family, friends, God, angels…) from whom you can draw support, strength, and sustenance?

❖ What signs show you that your support crew is present and helping you now?

❖ What leap of faith would you take today if you knew you were not alone?

Day 12

The Ink Floweth

The pen in hand,
But no ink.
The mechanics of writing,
Sure, I know how,
But I'm still not taking action
Because I can only see
A word or two ahead,
And not the final lay of the land.

This holds me in sentences.
Now and then comes a paragraph,
Sometimes even a blog post
Whizzed out in the eleventh hour.
But it's disjointed,
Not a whole,
Complete,
Flowing
Book.

What would it take
To allow the ink to flow
As it may?

What would it take
To have crystal-clear clarity,
Or at least feel a degree of comfort
In the way it emerges?

What would it take
To trust that the technical things
Can be easily sorted?

These are just mere details,
Yet my message
In its entirety
Is still kept invisible
Because of such
Distrust,
Lack of clarity,
Lack of focus.

What would break open the flesh of this book
And allow its guts
To be revealed
In all of her glory,
Untamed,
Unedited,
And even a little messy
And out of rhythm?

What would allow this book
To move from conception,
Gestation,
And finally birth after
Many miscarried attempts?

We do not alter the course of gestation.
We go with where it leads
And naturally grows,
And forms itself
Into beautiful form
To be birthed when ready.

We nourish ourselves well
During this phase,
Knowing that the baby
Grows without our volition,
But by a moving force
And energy within
That propels itself into beingness
In its own perfect timing,
With midwife on hand
And the support crew waiting
To witness the birth,
To celebrate the new life,
And to wonder at its
Creation,
Purpose,
Message to the world.

So why am I haltering
The spirit of this baby from coming
Into tangible form?
Truth be known,
I am scared of being a bad mother.

❖ How are you allowing or not allowing your creativity to shine? What keeps you stuck?

❖ What steps can you take today to get past those sticking points and create new momentum?

❖ How will you engage with your spirit, soul helpers, or support crew to help you bring your creative dreams into fruition?

Day 13

Conception Moon

In full light,
The conception moon
Dazzles down,
Hoping to spotlight
That which is to be seen
More of in the world.

To seed in magic
That creates cells,
That multiply
And take form.

To fertilise
So that bud becomes flower
And pod becomes fruit.

Full moon,
You potentise the air
With excitement
And sometimes restlessness.
A "full of the joys of spring" feeling
When we feel like
We are in our prime,
All systems go
And ready to take on the world

With new clarity,
Enlightenment,
Lightness,
Vim.

Arousal heightened,
Energy higher.
Surrounded by people,
And goals that desire
Fruitioning.

I am ready,
I am light
And lit up.
I no longer stand invisible,
As I now choose the spotlight
To show me the stage,
Not the shadows,
And to shine the way
On my movements,
My character,
And on the lead role,
I auditioned for:
My most important role,
And that is to play me
In all of my glory.

- ❖ What dream, goal, or project would you love to achieve?
- ❖ What ideas or decisions would you like more light shed on so that they can come to fruition?
- ❖ What specific steps will you take today to move you from dreaming about an idea to it becoming real?

Full Moon—Fire—Summer

"I let the fire within me fuel my passion to live a more lit up life."

The Creation Moon at Her Fullest

Burning Flame of Desire

Tarred and Feathered

Uncaged Life Story

My Chosen Kindred Mamas

Mothering the Child Within

The Silent Space

Voice of the Inner Critic

Day 14

The Creation Moon at Her Fullest

I riff from my heart,
Feel it in my soul,
Tell my story,
Reveal my heart,
And show up
Under the spotlight
And loving arms
Of She,
The creative mama
At her fullest.

Dancing in her own full moon light,
The full moon
Allows me to shine the spotlight
On the adventurous spirit of me
Standing on the cliff's edge of my past
And stepping into the unknown,
Where my heart
Beats, pumps, roars, cries,
And engages with others, heart to heart.

From years of feeling alone,
I whisper to you,
"You are not alone,"
And help you see the fullness of that truth.

From years of grief,
I remind you that life has a crazy way
Of ebbing and flowing,
And you will be okay.
I will help carry you from those turbulent waters
To one where the full moon is clear on the calm water,
Spotlighting the why of that experience
And the fullness that grief-filled time has brought you.

From years of pursuits and tick-off lists
In order to feel validated,
I remind you that you are already enough,
Even when you are doing nothing.

From divorce and time on my own without partner,
I remind you that you must love yourself
To allow another to be with you fully—
Not a half moon relationship,
But a full one in all of her glory.

From humbling in the money stakes,
And feeling the bones of my arse poking through,
And somehow managing to put another meal on the table
For my young family,
I remind you that you will always be provided for.
Sustenance in these moments
Often comes from the soul.

From finding not one but a few soulmates,
Where I recognised them instantly
And chose to be with them
For the time and reason allocated by spirit,
I want you to know that we are here
For a time, season, and reason of
Rich growing,

Self-expansion,
And a road to more
Self-love,
Self-acceptance,
And learning to step more into
The "foolness" of the moon,
Of the unknown of relationships
And what they teach us,
What adventures they bring us,
And what joy and pain they enable us to feel.

Creative mama,
Full moon,
You know how I have hidden in the shadows
For self-preservation
Out of not-good-enoughness,
And sometimes out of survival.
My heart so desires to be seen in my fullness,
To dance in the moonlight once again with more joy,
And to swim in her reflection
In the cool, clear waters of clarity,
And to be the fool
Trusting that when I fully follow my heart's desires,
I will totally be in my fullest feminine power,
And others will experience that love, self-belief,
Hope, peace, and joy for themselves
As my heart pines and reminds them they can also
Dance in their own full moonlight
Once again.

- ❖ Which of your life experiences can you use to help others see light in their dark times?
- ❖ What talents are you hiding which, when brought out into the light, could make a real difference in the world?
- ❖ If you were to light the way for one other person today, who would that be, and what would you say or do?

Day 15

Burning Flame of Desire

Dare to leap forth into my desires,
My destiny,
My day-to-day life
As I am being called.

If I were to feel the ouch
That comes from touching the fire of desire,
And knowing I can manifest all that I have dreamed about
Yet have been scared of,
Let me tear open my fear,
Throw her in the fire
With wild abandonment,
And dance around the fire
In full swing of what manifests.

My fire of desire
Creates written and spoken words
That reach the heart of people
And show them a new compass
That will navigate them
Into less turbulent waters
And into the soothing waters of love.

My fire of desire
Has me walking the sometimes rocky
And difficult road beside people

Hand in hand,
Easing their blisters
And urging them on when they want to give up.
We travel together,
We retreat together,
We heal together
And we walk a simpler path.

My fire of desire
Allows me to travel to far-off places,
Yet places that draw me in
Like they're calling me home,
And into familiar territory
So I need not fear
What my mission is there.
The mission is clear
And it is pure love in action.

My fire of desire
Allows me expressions of creativity
That fuel me,
Soothe me,
Heal me and others
As we dance, paint,
Create, celebrate,
Heal, desire,
And manifest.

My fire of desire
Gifts me freedom from motherhood
As I have known it.
Yet my deepest desire
Is deep respect and love
From those whom I have loved beyond measure.
If I died tomorrow,

That would be my deepest longing.

My fire of desire
Gifts me abundant currency
To support, sponsor,
And be the ambassador
Of someBODY BEAUTIFUL
There for women
Who also wish to step up
And flourish in self-love,
Body honouring,
Soul nourishment,
Femininity,
And connection to spirit.

My fire of desire
Has me dancing around the fire
With other creative, intelligent, and caring souls
Whose calling is also that of love.
Our collective skills and talents
Allow our work not to be hard,
But instead to be uplifting, empowering,
Life changing,
Not zapping us of energy
But energising us
Where we too feel hammocked
In support, love, and courage.

My fire of desire
Asks me to honour my closest relationship with my love,
To have time, space, and continued openness,
To grow
And experience the warmth, excitement, and love
From the spark that comes from
Pure intimacy,

Sensuality,
Soul connection,
With one other.

My fire of desire
Gifts me opportunities
To speak across the divide of language
Through deepening my own language skills,
And opening the opportunities
To minister, create and enjoy life with people
In other languages,
Countries,
Communities.

My fire of desire
Is for my life to be one of immense pleasure:
Food, wine, social occasions,
Great lovemaking,
Physical challenges,
Travel,
Entertainment,
Soul-satisfying pleasures.

My fire of desire
Throws away fear,
Self-doubt,
Past failures,
Procrastination,
Lack of clarity,
Responsibility,
Obligation,
Fear of judgement
Or not-good-enoughness,
No money,
Lack of momentum,

Going it alone,
Hiding out,
And whatever else
Conscious or unconscious
That has hindered my fire
To burn,
And my light to shine,
And my path to be easy.

My fire of desire
Now pleads
To transform my desire
Into tangible manifestations
That leave me in that feeling of awe
And immense gratitude.

- ❖ What desires have you extinguished in the past and want to reignite?
- ❖ What are your new burning flames of desire?
- ❖ What do you intuitively feel will fuel those desires and help them manifest?

Day 16

Tarred and Feathered

I got in touch today
To ask them
Why had they done what they had done?
Something that felt like the biggest betrayal ever,
That has caused my flesh
To still be
Open,
Raw,
Festering,
Yet unaddressed,
Hidden beneath
Some cotton wool
As nobody acknowledges
Or nurses the seeping wound
For fear of opening the wound even more.

Ouch!
Not prepared to reply to my question,
Which was shut down,
Unanswered,
And unapologised for.

She wished me well for my healing
But would not take responsibility
For what she had done that had caused
My bleeding wound,

Which stings even more today
As I have again exposed it.

The other continues to encourage me
In my mothering,
But never did an apology come
For the decision
That has had such an impact on my life.

Sometimes we need
To let go of the attachment to people
Who are our biggest
Unbelievers,
Judges,
Perpetrators of untruth
Which they would like
To harness as
The truth
Of who we really are.

It is even more painful
Because of the thread
Of pink bloodline
From not just one side,
But the outlaw side as well
Who have at times ostracized,
Thrown stones,
And pulled me along the street tarred and feathered.

It hurts,
It stings,
It burns,
It goes deep.

But they do not know me fully,
And I am not who they see me as.

Underneath those feathers,
I am mother love.

❖ What impact has others' judgement of you had on your life?

❖ Where does lack of forgiveness sit in your body?

❖ Who are you truly underneath the layers of how people perceive you?

Day 17

Uncaged Life Story

Caged no more,
And yes, she will sing.

My new role in life
Is standing on the stage
Accoladed,
Validated,
Crowned for being me
In my extraordinariness,
Not booed at by the crowd
Or concert unattended.
Taking the lead role,
Not sitting in the shadows,
But being warmly received
Because I have touched
The very heart
Of those that watch, listen, and grow.

My new story
Has me being storyteller
And the compassionate listener,
Rather than the advisor,
Coach,
Solution finder.
I listen to the stories

And help lessen someone's load,
Ease her pain and suffering,
And allow her
To see the unravelling
Of love in her life,
And the new, exciting possibilities
That come from that heart space.

My new stories in life
Are travelling tales.
I travel even more,
But this time more resourced financially
So I can indulge in
More pleasure,
More opportunities,
More freedom
To open to where spirit
Asks me to be,
To honour my calling
Skills, talents, interests
On the road
And share with those
Who need them,
And whose offerings I need
For mutual growth and enjoyment.

In my new romance novel,
I enjoy my love
In partnership
Not as an addition to my family and their needs,
But finally as a couple,
Complete,
Two.

My new sport in the game of life
Is not one of playing tennis
With me on one side
And the others on the other.
It is me
Playing team tennis
Not out to win,
But to enjoy the game
For its pleasure,
In collective
Spirit,
Support,
And fun together.

My life's location
Is not in big cities.
It journeys me into nature,
Stillness,
And deeper relationship
With Mother Earth and her fullness.
The moon follows me,
And I follow her.
The air is fresh,
Clean and clear.
My own head is clear.
The stream carries
My fears and tears away,
And soothes my soul,
And refreshes my body.
The fireplace
Beckons me to
Sit in her warmth
And burn
Old stuff
For constant renewal

Of my spirit,
My strength,
And joy of being alive.
It allows me to share stories
As we gather around the fire with ones we love.

My life with words
Is expanded beyond measure
And finds its way
Into homes,
Bookstores,
Women's circles,
Red tents,
Onto stages,
And even on the sand,
Where the written or spoken word
Is difficult to access.
It is multilingual,
Crossing the divide of language,
Culture,
Religion,
Thought.
I swim in words
Of many languages,
Loving the fluency
Of self-expression
That language offers me.

I also love that love
Does not need language.
Love is silent gorgeousness.

My culinary recipe book
Feeds me great delights
From many corners of the world

In far-off places,
But equally offers beautiful moments
Of sharing a table,
Communing
Sacredly,
At one with others.

My life story is also one of philanthropy,
Opening doors
To those who would love the chance
To step up,
Shine,
Be uncaged,
Unsilenced,
And liberated
Into living
More fully,
More at peace,
More creatively,
More joyfully,
And more on purpose,
Making their difference.

My body, her story,
Continues to be one of
Body gratitude,
Nourishment,
Tenderness,
Opening intimacy,
And kindness.
It finds its pleasure
In dance,
Sensuality,
Lovemaking,
Movement,

Grace and elegance,
And sometimes sweat.
And I finally discover
Restful sleep
And energised wake-ups
To allow me to
Fully be in the world
And her pleasures.

My new story
I leave to unfold
Unscripted,
With spirit
In full trust
And admiration
That the story
Reveals itself
Not just to be read,
But to be fully lived
And breathed.

- ❖ Which chapter of your life can you now view from a more empowered perspective?
- ❖ If you could write your life story, what would your next chapter have in it?
- ❖ If you lived your life with more depth, how would that look?

Day 18

My Chosen Kindred Mamas

My mother of birth;
Superwoman,
Perfectionist,
Keeper of the peace.
A busy woman,
Talented,
Skilled.
Woman of words,
Hands of creativity,
Generous heart.
Server of people,
Sacrificing self
For others.
Probably a means
Of keeping her
Validated within
While she often goes without.

Another mama,
My Nana Mary—
Oh, the fun we had together.
And the memories we collected
Were gone too soon.
I miss the coins she passed me
Quietly without notice,
Her way of saying she was proud of me.

I miss her lolly jar,
Overcooked cabbage,
Homemade quince jelly,
My sleepovers,
And my ventures through her jewellery box of brooches.
I miss her coming to watch me dance
Because she was ever so proud
Of the dancing spirit within me.

I felt she understood me.
She hugged me,
And kissed me,
With her hairy aging chin.
I was included in her market days
And shouted milkshakes at the corner milk bar.
But she was taken too soon and too suddenly.

The Saturday morning news of her death
That I was awoken to
Killed me.
Distraught,
Devastated,
Not wanting to believe
That special mama had gone.
The mama who I also heard
Was mama to many
Who were abandoned,
Neglected,
Ostracized,
Lost,
And had no place.

She truly was
The caring mama,
Heart mama

To us femmes
Whose fates
Lead us to feel
Self-doubting,
Different and alone,
And made us fight and fend for
Our worthiness
And place of belonging.

My mama-in-laws,
Yes, I had two
Because of the widower I married:
His mother-in-law
And his own mother.
One in grief for her lost daughter
Whom I would never measure up against.
I was not to be the mother of her grandchildren
And was not her daughter,
The precious one that did no wrong.
But that saintliness is often what is given
To those who pass early,
And whose fuller life has not been given
The means to be explored,
And character developed
Into something more
That may or may not be
Agreeable
In a mother's eyes.

The other,
Someone who felt her role of nana
Was taken away
By the capable me who came on board
Following the accident that left her grandchildren motherless.
She took on that mantle of motherhood

And lost it when I entered the picture,
Unintentionally taking the role from her
And assuming the mantle myself.

She had to bear her own pain
Of losing the validation she sought
By caring for her grandchildren through their grief.
And her angry arrow
Was thrown at me,
The target.
But she died soon after,
Leaving a trail of hurt saying
I was the worst mother on this planet.
That was her final judgement of me.

Aunty figures, sister figures, my own maternal line
Absent for many years now,
Bringing up my own six children without them.
I have not been blessed
With my tribe around me to call upon.
I have gone it alone,
And as I reflect on this,
I am saddened.
For it takes a village
To bring up a child.

I have done my best.
I have done very well.
But to the expense
Of my own well often feeling dry,
Often wishing I had a mama,
The aunty,
The sister,
The grandmother
Who would pick up the pieces,

Allow me to sleep now and then,
Allow me the freedom to go out,
Help me with decisions,
And help me refill my tank.

I honour other mamas
Who have heard me
Cry into the night,
Fed me when I was hungry,
Clothed me when I was cold,
Encouraged me when I was unbelieving,
Supported me when I went solo,
Gave me money when I was humbled,
And held my back
When others didn't.

I gather my own mamas around me,
Unrelated
But kindred spirits,
Not numerous
But those with mama hearts,
Those who genuinely care,
And those who show their love
In action:
Small but significant,
Little but loving,
Not out of feeling responsible
But out of pure love
For a kindred spirit mama,
Friend,
Woman.

- ❖ What part have mother figures played in your life?
- ❖ What has been your experience of mothering others?
- ❖ Who are your kindred spirit mamas, and who would you now like to gather in that circle?

Day 19

Mothering the Child Within

My days as a child,
I dreamed I was in Africa,
At the orphanages,
Living with kids
So they felt they had
Not just a home
But a family who cared
And who loved them.

When Lady Diana died,
I cried for weeks.
Not because of her death as such,
Although she was a beautiful mother figure to many,
But for the pain of her boys
And the growing up they had to do without her.

When I took on my three oldest
As young girls,
After the fatal accident of their birth mum,
I knew I was gifted them,
To nurse them through their grief
In the various transitions of their lives:
First missing tooth,
Birthdays,
New schools,

First boyfriends,
Graduation dances,
Uni celebrations,
Motherhood,
And successes
Without her.

The other three I birthed—
Delicious pregnancies,
Babies delivered healthy and thriving.
And as I have watched them grow
And develop their own little souls
Into now teenage bodies,
Dreams,
Characters,
Passions,
I am in some ways disappointed.
Their life was different than I imagined,
Having gone solo for some time,
And absent father in the shadows.
I cry for them
And smile for them
As I see their growing
Resourcefulness,
Independence,
And love for their world
And themselves.

I remember the funerals of babes
I have attended,
And the agony I felt
For the grieving mamas,
Not just because of their babes
Taken so early,
But of the years ahead

They would not have
With each other.

I remember the conversations I have had
With mothers who have lost
Their young ones to suicide:
Agony,
Bewilderment,
Guilt,
Regret,
Wondering.
And life goes on
Somehow.

I notice my own inner judgement
When mothers' time and attention
With their kids is sacrificed
For their own success in the world.
Yes, a judgement,
But I feel it in my soul,
And I feel it in the spirit of children
That this is wasted time
We would regret if we were to die today.

Let us love our children like no other day,
Lest we also not forget to
Mother ourselves fully
As a caring mother loves her child.

- ❖ How can you be a better mother to yourself?
- ❖ How can you be more present with people in your life today?
- ❖ What is the legacy of being a woman, mother, or lover that you wish to leave?

Day 20

The Silent Space

Who will guide me today
To write about the ritual of writing
My muse, my message, and my memes?

I flip open my book for assistance.
Serapis Bey—
Perfect.
Stop rushing.
You need to create
Silent space
To hear your inner voice
That desires a listening ear.

Much like a breastfed babe,
Be nourished by such connection
And feed at regular intervals,
So you don't go hungry or thirsty,
And you are sustained
As you share love
From your heart.

Make your voice be your
Utmost priority,
And in the stillness
Find that voice.

- ❖ How do you presently create stillness in your life?
- ❖ How could more time connecting with your inner spirit and nature benefit you?
- ❖ What is in your heart today that is asking to be voiced?

Day 21

Voice of the Inner Critic

I was not really taught
How to land on my feet by my family,
Because they shied away from telling me
What career path or passion to follow.
They said I would know,
But actually I didn't.

But I did have a big dream
To become a doctor;
I could help save the world.
But I could hear my critic saying,
"You're not smart enough"
Even though I topped the class every year.
I didn't become a doctor.

Occupational Therapy became my game,
Topping every level of study,
Only to fail once
In my third year.
Some assessor
Did not like my unique take on the subject
And gave me a low grade.
The gavel fell;
Depression set in.
Perhaps that was my starting point
Of silencing my unique voice.

I fell into my first role
With that ball and chain of critic at my feet,
But with some anticipation I could change that.

First paid job was in the psych ward
With those who were suffering.
Out of my league,
In my youth,
And lacking worldly life experience,
I struggled,
Unsupported by more experienced staff around me.
I treaded water,
Gasping sometimes for help,
Swimming against the tide,
But relating to the people with compassion.
But again, my unique way
Was squished,
Squashed,
And I left.
Overseas called me.

My overseas travel.
Yeah, to be free in the world.
Tour leader twenty-four seven.
Played every role possible,
But one piece of feedback destroyed me.
My critic
Sent me home
To nothing,
Depressed
And suicidal.

My critic was in full swing.
I picked myself up,
Dusted myself off,

And started all over again,
And found my means of service:
Supporting teens with babes.
Oh, I loved this,
Feeling in my element,
Loving the teaching, empowerment,
And inspiration I offered.
But I felt too young
And inexperienced,
As I was without child
Or the experience of motherhood.
Yes, I had life skills and wisdom
To teach these young women,
But my critic sent me packing.

I taught English to foreigners,
Again topping my class
And immediately being offered a job.
Great work, Janelle.
Many ticks,
Few crosses,
Until I was snapped up in marriage,
And I moved location
And into the realms of
Instant motherhood.
Yes, here I felt at home.

Many of my next years
Were spent with busy family:
Six kids, a husband,
And my career ambitions behind me,
Willingly taking on a more complimentary working role,
But honouring the full-time nature
Of motherhood,
Superwoman,

Doer unto others,
Excelling.
But critic,
My own
And others,
Sometimes hurt.

Going solo
And choosing that split.
Yes, the leaver is judged
More than the one who is left.
But he wouldn't make that call,
So I bore the brunt,
Knowing full well
The decision was the right one.
But this did not leave me in favour
Of those who were hurting.
I felt for their hurt,
But I felt my own pain too.
My critic reared her head,
But my gentle knowing
Kept me on my feet,
Even when I was walking
The humblest ground I had ever trod.

The expansion over recent years
Of stepping up into
Speaking, writing, events,
Healing, and personal growth
Has been exhilarating,
Scary,
Fulfilling,
Liberating,
Constraining,
Life directing,

And life stopping—
Easy and difficult.
Sure, with critic in tow,
But in a softer, gentler voice,
One that doesn't bash me up,
Knock me down for too long,
Or stop me in my tracks.

What's the difference?

Finding my inner source
That says,
You are enough.
Follow your calling,
Your path,
Your message,
Your love
In the way
That only you can do, and be
Not with critic as your companion,
But with love as your guide
To land on your feet
And walk strongly
On your path.

- ❖ What have you missed out on in life because of your harsh inner critic?
- ❖ What do you feel is your real calling or life purpose?
- ❖ How can you gently tame your inner critic so that you can begin to have more confidence and trust in yourself?

Waning Moon—Water—Autumn

"My tears could not put out the bonfire of leaves that were shed."

Not-Good-Enoughness Seeks Companion

Comfy Shoes and High Heels

The Bomb or the Bonfire

The Return

The Peacemaker and the Justice Fighter

Shape Shifting into Self

The Perfect Bloom

Day 22

Not-Good-Enoughness
Seeks Companion

I feel it deep within
My gut,
My not-good-enoughness.

My inner critic,
She also lies
In my sleeplessness,
Worrying about
What might be
And mightn't be.

She shows herself
In lack of clarity,
Jumbledness,
So my creation seldom comes
Fully together,
Fully to fruition,
Or fully experienced.
Sabotaged,
I miss out,
And others miss out.

But darling,
Could you not be my companion?

If I were just to hold you
And embrace you,
And allow you, my inner critic,
To hold my hand and accompany me,
Not bind me or hold me back,
But to walk with me
And gently prod me
Into stepping outside of my comfort zone
With more ease
And less worry,
Knowing that
As I am today,
I'm enough.
I'm a creation in progress,
And this is just fine.

And a reminder to my little girl self
To come out and play
Freely
Without worry,
Without fear,
Without confines.

The inner critic
Sits,
Stomps,
Stirs,
Stops.

My little girl
Plays,
Smiles,
Dances,
Sings.

The masculine critic,
The feminine little girl—
Could they not live happily together
Knowing each is a part of each other?

❖ Which of your childhood interests or passions would you like to recreate again?

❖ What areas of your life would you like to lighten up a little and have more fun in?

❖ What lifts your spirit and sings to your soul? How can you engage in that today?

Day 23

Comfy Shoes and High Heels

My comfy shoes,
My story,
My unique heart print.
Why else would I have gone through what I have,
If it were not to share my story
And help the reader?

My character loves the freedom
That comes from
Finally loving the skin she's in.
Yes, really in her skin
With so much comfort,
Joy even,
And a smile.
The unleashing from the cage
Of years of body loathing
To one of such freedom of body love is
Exhilarating,
Orgasmic even.
I know the paralysis of body loathing,
And now I dance with delight,
Moving more freely in my body
And truly loving her
For her magnificence.

My character is loving rocking through
The confines of self-doubt
That have raged within her for years in various guises:
Perfectionism,
Over-doing,
Control,
Sleeplessness,
Fatigue—
No, in fact
Burnout.
Actually, death of spirit.

She is moving through self-doubt
Not by banishing her
Or by cracking open a "let's get shit done" code
To prove she can do anything,
But by a gentle holding of her hand.
Self-doubt is learning to be her companion,
Not someone who leads her
And pulls her by her coat-tails,
Or pushes her onto a stage
To be accoladed
For her accomplishments and daring feats,
But quietly accompanies her and reminds her
Simply to find the confidence
To grow into who she truly is
And what she was born for.

My character is learning the joys of
Being her sensual, pleasure-seeking self,
From previously wearing
Religious,
Unexpressive,
Closeted,
Uncomfy shoes

Of controlled
Frigidity and unavailability.
She is free in her spirit,
Flowing in her feminine essence,
And finding her way home
To pleasure
Rather than pursuit
And piousness.

My character is learning
To take off the mask
That hides her raw feelings
And reveal more of her many sides,
Because the comfy shoes
Of only showing her kinder, more loving side
Actually confine her.
Her anger, resentment, jealousy,
Judgement, and shame
Are finding their voices,
Becoming unsilenced,
And unleashing themselves;
Sometimes not always comfy
For the wearer,
But definitely
Allowing her to
Be more real,
Feel
And
Reveal
Her fuller self,
And be true to others.

My character knows the claustrophobia
From wearing the mask
Of good-girlness and emotional restraint.

She is now curious and feeling her way
Into the unknown territory
Of rage,
Rawness,
Realness.

She has worn comfy shoes,
Familiar ones,
Sensible
And very worn-out,
And ones that have caged her,
Blistered her,
And kept her safe,
Sad,
Restrained.

She now adorns her gorgeous heels
And chooses freedom,
Pleasure,
Self-care,
And true expression
To be her dance partner.

- ❖ What, or who has confined, restrained, and kept you in a life that you don't enjoy?
- ❖ What pleasures have you denied yourself of over the years?
- ❖ What new pleasures would you like to discover, free of the restraints and taboos of your past?

Day 24

The Bomb or the Bonfire

Enraged,
This morning I wake.
In fact, woken
Not out of slumber,
But from a restless night.
Awake,
Pissed, in fact,
That my huge smile
Of contentment and joy
Last night as I lay me down to sleep
Was wiped off my face
By one's blow.
Not a physical one,
But one that fuelled my fire
And ignited me.

My greatest joy
Comes from hearing contented,
Joy-filled children,
My children
When they light up like a Christmas tree,
Summer here in New Zealand,
Enjoying both the anticipation and enjoyment
Of fun-filled family times.

My youngest are teens now,
And they lit me up
As they entered the house
Late last night
After a long, metaphorical winter,
But emerging out of their night
With the joys of spring:
Laughter,
Togetherness,
And great times had by all
In their steps.

Only to be harshly interrupted by
The accent,
The words,
And the views
Of someone who doesn't seem to love hearing
Joy-filled children
Fill the house.
He only imagined life with me,
Not my kids.
Enraged,
Sad,
Sorrow,
And feeling like autumn leaves
Are falling,
Being gathered
Perhaps
To build a bonfire.

I don't know,
But maybe I do.

❖ How is relating to someone close to you difficult because of your different values?

❖ What could you do to find a better balance between honouring your values and needs and those of others?

❖ What brings you joy, and how can you continue to live in joy daily?

Day 25

The Return

My son,
My son.
Oh, how I have missed you,
Having graciously let you go
Where you needed to go,
And not where I wanted you to be:
Safe in my heart,
Under my wing,
And in my embrace
Of mother love.

The pain
That you are now adult,
And I have missed some years
Of you becoming that man,
Walking the rite of passage
Into such extraordinary
And sometimes difficult times
Of emerging manhood.

My pain of womanhood,
Being a mother,
Simply wanting to make your way
Easier,
Brighter,
And with a softer landing,

To hold and rock you so you feel secure,
Is entwined somewhat with my own deep desire
To feel needed, wanted, and respected.

On your short return,
I feel intense sadness
That I have missed those few years.
And I notice it even more intensely
Than when you were absent from our home.
Your return has rifted my heart
And reminded me of that pain
Of letting you sail into unknown waters,
And reminded me
Of how powerless I have felt
To be the mama
I wanted me to be,
Not what you needed me to be.

But as I shed buckets of tears
Into my well this morning,
Which has for some time now
Felt dry,
I am filled with more sustenance,
Admiration,
Pride,
And motherly love
Of the way
You are becoming the man
You were destined to be,
And the path you have walked,
Which may not have been
The trail I planned for you,
But one that has shown you the way
To who you are today.

You have done well, my son,
Minus me
In the past few years.

And my cup runneth over
With respect for myself too,
For the foundations I set,
The seeds I planted,
The water of love I sprinkled,
And the ever-constant knowingness—
Not an easy one,
But an important one:
That it is not a mother who determines
How a seed grows
As much as she would like to think this.
The seed himself grows
With his own knowingness
Inside.

- ❖ What change, loss or challenge has caused you grief?
- ❖ How is your grief showing itself or how are you hiding it?
- ❖ What creative activity could help you fully experience your grief and allow you to heal?

Day 26

The Peacemaker and the Justice Fighter

One person, not that respectful at present
Of my needs and those of the kids,
Someone who lives at a distance,
Who appears all soft, gooey, and calm,
Saying those words,
Sounding less than convincing,
But out of sheer exasperation
And hope
That finances will get better soon.
But not really actioning his butt off
To change things,
Or be there for the kids.
Or it seems so from the judgement chair
Where I sit,
Feeling saddened.

How long can a woman wait,
Wait,
And wait some more
Through the peaceful expression and sounds
Of such promises long overdue?

The other
Out for justice
At all costs,
Straight to the jugular,
Heart out of the equation,
Mind in action,
Body in fighter stance,
Teeth ready to bite,
And a winning
"Get this shit sorted now"
Grip in his hands,
Ready to wring someone's neck
If it's not sorted
His way
And in his timing.

The taste of caramel
Is alluring,
Delicious,
Sweet,
But it can burn.
And as I continue to chew on caramel
And see the good side,
Sit in my patience chair,
And continue to chew the same lolly,
And allow him to walk over me,
And ignore my needs
And those of the kids.
It is far from peaceful in my spirit,
It is far from sweet in my gut,
It is far from love,
Fairness,
And justice in my heart.

But it is I who continues
To choose caramel
And notice its deliciousness,
Not its ability to burn.

And on the other side of the ring
Is Mr. Justice Fighter,
Boxing gloves on,
Having fought this fight before
And determined to conquer
His quest,
His opponent,
His own intention.
And as a fighter in the ring,
One does not consider the other person.
His soul aim is to put his opponent
Out of the game
And put himself
In the ring as the winner.
He calls it self-respect.

The justice fighter
Is irked by my patience
And compassionate ear
For the peacemaker's strife.
My nature, however, is not to fight,
But to have understanding
And a more win-win heart.
But this devalues me
As I continue to put me down the list
And allow the peacemaker to continue,
To quietly sit in his stuff
And have that influence
Me and my life.

And as much as I no longer love the peacemaker,
And I claim to love the justice fighter,
The fighter is becoming
Less attractive in this moment too,
For his words are too harsh a blow
On my delicate skin.
Yes, I know he is teaching me
To fight for justice
For the purpose of my own
Self-value,
Deservedness,
And wholeness,
But he's punching me into the ground
With his right hook.

Or perhaps I simply need to learn to fight
And see that my own peacemaking
By tolerating without boundaries
Can cause internal warfare
That will one day
Kill.

- ❖ What have each of your relationships gifted you even if they have ended?
- ❖ How does keeping the peace impact you and others positively and negatively?
- ❖ What boundaries would you like to set in your current relationships?

Day 27

Shape Shifting into Self

Pushed into corners
And constraints of my busy diary,
Schedules,
Things to do list,
And "be all to everyone" mentality
Has, over many years,
Shaped me into something
I don't want to be:
Superwoman.

Not so super any longer, however,
Because exhaustion
Doesn't help me
Live with vibrancy,
Joy,
Or truly just be me.

It's a cardboard cut-out of me,
So shaped by my own expectations
From within,
The imprisonment of
Time,
Schedule,
Templating.
Looking like everyone else,
Succeeding in life their way

That by most is seen as the norm,
Desired,
Or a mark of success.
It's squashing me
And keeping me 2D.

But I don't fit in those circles
Of women who cling onto
The next three secret principles
Of doing well in biz,
Or the latest blueprint for
Having the life they love.
I don't fit in those gatherings
Where it's the exclusive club
For the latest and greatest aspiring
Entrepreneurs or success-driven women
Who shape themselves into
A busy, tight diary,
Workload,
And social commitment.
I cry for what they are missing out on
In their pursuit for freedom
That they dream will come
One day.

I often stand alone,
Feeling like I'm a triangle,
While others are squares
Wanting to be bigger
And better squares.

My greatest desire is to be the
Flowingly,
Fabulously,
Fun-fulfilled

Me again
Who doesn't get shaped
By such imprisonment
But craves for me
In all my shapeless glory
That once was,
To re-emerge.

My desire
Is to feel successful in the moments
I take care of me and not always others,
When I don't appear to have anything
Or I don't appear to be moving anywhere.

There is true success
And contentment,
Feeling peaceful
In my humblest,
Darkest,
And even messiest place
As a woman,
Where I am not
The 2D cardboard that's monochrome
But instead a 3D,
Mutable,
Colourful
Un-shape.

But it takes something to shape shift into self,
To metamorph
And know
That my greatest success is to
Frolic in the sea of difference,
Not float in the sea of sameness;
To flow with my own rhythmic nature,

Rather than march to the beat of someone else's drum;
To love my curves of my body, my life, my cycle,
And not be the straight-line pursuit driven women
Who drives and strives
At the same pace every day
While missing out on the scenery on the way;
And to be messy and vulnerable
Joyful and pleasured,
A non-chameleoned woman
Who has the freedom of
Not camouflaging herself.

❖ What expectations are you living into that don't align with who you truly are?

❖ What is the cost of you "fitting the mould" or living life inauthentically?

❖ What is one step you will take today to break out of that mould?

Day 28

The Perfect Bloom

No rose is the same,
Even though she may resemble
Other roses who share her bush.

Her petals
Are in perfect order,
Different from the others.
Her thorns
Are uniquely hers.
She buds and blooms in her own
Divine timing,
And her scent
Wafts in the proportions
And timing
That make her
The perfect
Rose.

Which other roses
Do I admire,
See in their fullest beauty,
Soak in their scent,
And pick to enjoy
Put in my favourite vase,
Or give as a beautiful gift to a friend?

Christiane Northrup:
A woman of immense
Knowledge,
Medical and energetic.
Helping women
To reconnect to their
Women's bodies,
Women's wisdom.

Lisa Lister:
The menstrual maven
Whose words sing to my soul,
And whose subject
Makes total sense
And riffs in my veins
And lights the path for women
To finally be women,
Messy and all.

Anita Johnston:
The storyteller
Who sinks us into our unconscious minds
To eat in the light of the moon,
Heal our eating wounds,
And acknowledge the intuitive,
Feminine,
Inner voice
That wants to be unsilenced.

Maya Angelou:
Phenomenal woman
With joy in her feet.
Poetess,
Activist,
Word priestess

Whose words - powerful and honest,
Have inspired millions
To become uncaged
And sing again.

Mother Teresa:
Role modelled
Love in action,
Reminding us that what we are doing
Is just a drop in the ocean.
But the ocean would be less
Because of that missing drop.
Her simple words and actions
She lived by
And made a profound difference
In the lives of many.

Oriah Mountain Dreamer:
Has made an invitation
To millions
To reach into their souls
And listen to their inner landscape,
To dance,
To take on the call,
And to live fully.

Dawna Markova:
Who will not die an unlived life,
Reminds me to feel
The wind in my hair,
The whispers of my heart,
The awakenings of my soul,
And to live divided no more.

This collective of women,
And other phenomenal women
Who have graced my path,
Have all used their voices,
Their words,
Their hearts
To be in their truth,
Their power,
Themselves.

Beautiful roses,
All unique,
Sharing the same garden.

- ❖ Who are the collective of people who have inspired, encouraged and offered you their wisdom?
- ❖ Who have you helped, influenced and made a difference to?
- ❖ Who do you now wish to connect with to further your life's purpose?

Dark Moon Return—Earth—Winter

"In winter, she came home to her hearth and warmed herself."

Step into My Pause

Love Letter to Self – Je t'aime

Coming Home – Jahmaya

Day 29

Step into My Pause

It's time to step into my pause,
Thin space between spirit and myself.
Time to do nothing today
As I await the new moon.

❖ How are you with simply "being in the pause" and doing nothing?
❖ What message did you hear in your spirit today?
❖ What steps will you take to honour that intuitive message?

Day 30

Love Letter to Self – Je t'aime

Je t'aime, ma chérie.
I speak love to you
From all of the goddesses,
Gorgeous women,
Great inspirationesses,
Gifted poetesses,
And girls in soul,
Who love you
And yearn for you
To continue to be
The great mama,
Matriarch,
Visionary,
Gift of compassion and inspiration
To other women.

To finally find
And fuel their feminine;
To fiercely love themselves,
Their bodies,
Their ebb and flow,
And to be fully women
As they navigate their transitions in life.

Je t'aime.
I love you
And remind you
To live with pleasure,
Live with joy,
And also honour your sadness
Your self-doubt,
Your niggling voice within.
For it's the waxing and waning,
Vulnerability and victory,
Sexy and sacred,
That make you
Whole,
Complete,
Human.

Je t'aime, my dear.
I honour you, my beautiful body,
For feeling this raw pain,
Noticing the hurt within it walls,
And the desire to quit,
But letting its slow release
Heal your wounds,
Comfort your bruises,
And be released
In flow
For a new day.

You don't need to hold
The pain of your past,
Your lineage,
Your lost love
Within.
Allow it to
Fly from the cage

And set you free.
Let it flow,
Let it flow,
Let it flow.

Je t'aime.
I'm sorry
For wasted years of not
Loving and honouring
Your gorgeousness.
My child, you are gifted.
You danced,
Wrote,
Played
Before grief grabbed you
And invisibility set in.
Joy dissipated,
And self-sufficiency
Became your familiar.
Dance again,
Write words,
And pleasure yourself
With more joy,
For that is your life lesson.

Je t'aime.
Be grateful for the women
Who have hurt you.
They have been your teachers,
Navigators,
And sideline cheerers,
Jeerers,
Leerers,
To help you shape your inner resolve
To believe in you.

Je t'aime.
To you, my body,
Which I treated as an enemy,
Archrival,
And thing to hate for so long.
I am in wonder
Of your resilience,
Patience.
Brilliance.
I marvel at your beauty,
Strength of character,
And forgiving nature.
Je t'aime,
Je t'aime,
Je t'aime.

- ❖ What are you going to write today in your love letter to self?
- ❖ What regrets can you now use positively to have an even better life?
- ❖ What are you grateful to your body for? How will you show your gratitude?

Coming Home – Jahmaya

At the beginning of this journey following the phases of the moon and the cycle of Mother Nature, I knew I was going somewhere profound. It is the moon that has illuminated the path that has led me to honour and love who I truly am, where I have been, and who has been important in my soul's journey to date.

My spiritual name has revealed herself as Jahmaya, and she has started breathing life into me more fully. She has always been there, but I feel her power even more strongly today.

Jahmaya,
Jahmaya,
Jahmaya.
Great mother,
Matriarch,
Midwife,
Wise woman,
Brave warrioress,
Feminine divinity,
Goddess,
She who brings increase,
Close to God.
I let her swirl
Through my veins,
Melt her into my heart,
Breathe her into my lungs,
Feel her vibration,
And smile
At her coming home.

Conclusion

Curvaceous Moon

Let's face it. Women are curves and not straight lines.

Our bodies are beautifully curvaceous.
Our minds are multitasking wonders.
Our emotional states fluctuate.
Our souls flow as we learn our life lessons.
And our lives are filled with curveballs.

But we are told to dislike, disown, or distrust our curves.

The masculine aspect of us only approves when we are "thin enough" and "beautiful enough," and we undertake rigid regimes to ensure that. We have also been taught to manage our menstruation, menopause, and body mayhem as if they were problems to be sorted, rather than listen to our bodies' inherent wisdom and allow the factors underlying our problems to be revealed and healed.

We listen to our logic and get bombarded with an overload of information to help us make decisions, solve a problem, or help us through a challenge, rather than honour our feminine intuition and soul-knowing, which pave an easier and more natural way to wellness and happiness.

We are told to contain, harness, resist or keep a lid on our emotions – showing only ones that are "appropriate". And we keep our "I've got it together mask" on to show that we are coping in the world when in reality we are not. The feminine in us is crying out for all of our emotions to be felt, expressed and heard and for us to be comfortable with our fluctuating emotional state. That is being fully woman.

Society's requirements for us to move through the linear stages of having the house, the kids, the career, and other markers of success are prioritised over what are soul yearnings are begging us to be, do, and have. A diary, template, and tick-off list is the masculine. A soul nourishment menu is the feminine.

The curveballs in our lives are considered time-wasters, distractions, nuisances, unfair, or failures. They could be seen as detours to a far more fulfilling journey or destination. The feminine knows there is always the perfect reason and season for everything, and it trusts in that perfection and surrenders to it.

Gorgeous women. As a collective and individually, it is time to honour our feminine. It is time to love our cycles. It is time to love what the moon, nature, and our menstrual cycle teach us about balancing the masculine and feminine so that we become whole, balanced, and well. It is time we have self-love and body honouring as a way of being. It is time to honour the calling of our hearts and souls. And we are being extended an invitation back to love through our feminine.

But how?

We all want the joys of spring and summer, but the darkness of our literal and metaphorical winter is also important, and so too is the shedding of stuff that is no longer wanted or needed in autumn. The masculine is about regime, routine, and rigidity. The feminine is honouring and aligning our rhythms with nature's seasons and monthly and daily cycles, and being in flow with them rather than fighting against them. Ritual is an important way of honouring the seasons within us.

The goal-focussed, energetic, out there doing life, biz, and juggling-a-zillion-things-at-once part of our menstrual cycle needs to be balanced with the second phase of our cycle, which yearns for more solitude, less busyness, and more rest, relaxation, and reflection. The masculine would have us doing the same stuff day in and day out. The feminine asks for fluctuation to enable us to enjoy better women's health and wellness - physically, mentally, emotionally, relationally, sexually and soulfully. The feminine also reminds us that is okay to stop, withdraw, and do nothing—without guilt.

Nature is pining for us to spend more time with her, rather than sitting in the confines of our material world. Mother Earth and the moon are our feminine, asking us to be grounded caretakers of ourselves and the world, and to be our gorgeous, emotional and compassionate selves. Father Sky and the sun are the masculine, asking us to hold the vision, apply the action, and make hay while the sun shines.

The feminine is asking us to be more authentic, real, and honouring of ourselves, rather than tiptoeing around people and doing what we think is expected of us. The feminine is unmasked and vulnerable. She becomes more comfortable with occasionally hurting someone, saying something that may well offend, or doing something for herself over and above others. She does what her soul is asking of her even if that means letting someone down. This is not selfishness; it is self-care and self-love.

The masculine aspect is the thick-walled artery that pumps out blood from the heart under high pressure in order to supply the body with oxygen and nutrients. It is the giver, and we women are so used to operating from this masculine space. The feminine aspect is the vein, smaller than an artery, and drains blood from the body and allows the heart to receive again for another cycle to begin. Our literal and metaphorical heart requires giving and receiving to be the best heart it can be. The art of receiving is yours to learn.

And on a daily basis, the feminine is yearning for still time and connection with your inner spirit. Discover yourself beyond your day-to-day working demands and responsibilities. Allow your inner spirit to be your guide. That guidance, support, and peace will come from your stillness space and place that you create daily.

So, gorgeous, I trust that both this poetry and the reflections will allow you to dance in your own full moonlight again and be fully woman in your ebb and flow, and lead you down the path of more self-love.

Acknowledgements

First, I acknowledge the luscious Lisa Lister www.thesassyshe.com who was my shining light as I wrote and, in her words, "spilled my guts" over the period of thirty days through the moon phases.

I also honour the many other women—writers, poets, storytellers, visionaries, doctors, and healers—who have been my rock as I have been at dead-ends, detours, and new direction points in my life. The women I specifically mention in my poetry are these gorgeous, wise women.

Christiane Northrup	www.drchristianenorthrup.com
Anita Johnston	www.dranitajohnston.com
Maya Angelou	www.mayaangelou.com
Mother Teresa	www.motherteresa.org
Oriah Mountain Dreamer	www.oriah.org
Dawna Markova	www.dawnamarkova.com

Others to whom I am incredibly grateful are my girlfriends, women whom I have coached and been part of their healing, audiences and workshop participants, men and women whose every word and insight I have devoured, and people who have seen, heard, and supported me at my highest and lowest.

I also thank my circle of women in soul, especially Ani and Nana Mary, goddesses and the feminine energy of spirit. They helped me re-engage in my daily stillness practice, connect to my essence, and channel these words for you to be uplifted and encouraged by.

Resources

As a speaker, writer, poet, and wise woman, I would love to share my womanly wisdom at your retreat, gathering, online summit, blog, or event—any avenue that honours and empowers women, children and families.

www.janellefletcher.com

Current Products and Services

Revive Your Feminine Spirit—Intuitive Women's Mentoring
Blog and Interview Series—A Woman's Rite of Passage to Self-Love
Somebody Beautiful Women's Circle
Rite of Passage Ceremonies
Speaker and MC
Events
Poetry

Facebook Communities

- Somebody Beautiful
- Dancing in Her Own Full Moonlight Women's Circle

Books Available on Amazon

- *The Light Within: A Collection of Peace and Prose*—My poem is "The Roar of the Lion Soul"
- *The Peacemakers: Restoring Love in the World through Stories of Compassion and Wisdom*—A compilation book. My chapter is "The Cyclical Wave of Soul—Why I Wasn't a Failure Leaving My Marriage."

Upcoming Products and Services

- A Beautiful Woman Series of Inspirations
- Reinvent Yourself and What's Possible Series
- Somebody Beautiful Retreats

About the Author

Hello, beautiful. I'm Janelle Fletcher. People describe me as a vibrant, creative, intuitive woman of courage who loves helping women believe in their gorgeousness and giftedness, and shine in their unique way. Anything that gets women out of their shell, comfort zone, or old story and reinvent who they think they are and what's possible is what I'm about.

- I have always been a teacher at heart. I help women become their own wise teachers.
- I have always felt for those who feel different and who feel they have no place of belonging. I help women find home within themselves.

- I ache within my soul for those who have lost others. It comes naturally to me to sit with them and connect them with those souls.
- I love acting on my intuition and expanding that gift. I help women honour their voice, their rhythms, and their soul whisperings.
- I cry with people in their dark times. I sit comfortably with people in that dark space and help lead them through that tunnel into light.
- I delight when people find new self-belief and step into their fullest power. I hold a great vision for women and help them create new ways, courage, and purpose to live their life more soulfully, simply, and on purpose.
- I find solace, creativity, and inspiration in connecting with spirit, and I know nothing more powerful, comforting, and supportive than faith and trust in my magnificence within. I help women revive and connect with their own inner spirits.

As a charitable soul and vibrant speaker, teacher, and wise woman, I shine on the stage as a leader of workshops or retreats, or as a front person or organiser for an event.

I am always creating new projects and ways to be of best service to women. From Revive Your Feminine Spirit intuitive women's mentoring to fun events for fabulous females; to writing articles, blogs, and poetry; to online self-care programmes, my well is full of delicious sustenance, inspiration, and support for you!

When I'm not helping others to honour themselves, I love family get-togethers, food and wine with my French partner, learning languages, watching cultural movies and uncovering more of my spiritual path.

I have run the New York marathon despite not being a runner and completed the 100km Oxfam event—just two of the many charity fundraisers which I have actively supported and participated in. I have travelled the world with my six children, sky-dived out of a plane after supporting kids living with cancer have that same opportunity, and I enjoy simple pleasures and non-run-of-the-mill living. I have twice been a guest speaker at the Game Changer Global Summit - the largest personal and spiritual online summit in the world - alongside many of the world's most renowned speakers, authors, healers, and sages. My writing is beginning to flourish and is touching the souls of many.

My global vision is to be ambassador of a cause that honours, educates, and empowers women, girls and families, and to continue travelling the world while living simply, loving well, and showing people the way to find their own light.

Printed in the United States
By Bookmasters